Carrie —

Make others "feel loved" they
can "get loved" anywhere —

All the Best

The Chronicles of
SIR VIVAL
Customer Service Under Siege

Joan Fox
www.feelserved.com

Edited by Gerdean O'Dell Bowen
Cover design and layout by www.TheBookProducer.com
Internal graphics designed by Amy Winegardner and Matt Hall
Printed in the United States of America

Joan Fox
The Chronicles of Sir Vival:
Customer Service Under Siege

ISBN 978-0-9797880-0-0
Library of Congress Control Number: 2007932735

Mailing Address
Cooper & Holman Publishers
PO Box 42754, Cincinnati, OH 45242

*This book is dedicated
to my brother Jack,
whose entrepreneurial spirit
ignited my own.*

Acknowledgements

To my family – Chuck, Chris, Andy, Erin, Maura and Cathy. You are the core that nurtures, inspires and drives me. I love you.

To the group of busy professionals and friends who cared enough to review the text of this book – in some cases multiple times – and contributed the insights that made this work better, thank you is not enough. Your generosity and loyalty overwhelm me.

Special thanks to Debbie Adams, Stephen Boyd, John Campbell, John Dodsworth, Katherine Forsythe, Barbara Glanz, Mel Gravely, Andy Hawking, Mark Hester, Patti Holmes, Bob Kramer, Scott Neltner, Kim Smith, Kensey Stedman, John Wagner, and Otis Williams.

Special Appreciation

A special thank you to my supporters in this project – you are "difference makers." Thank you for being the never-failing role models of what customer service can be.

• • • • •

"Much has been written about customer service but nothing comes close to Joan Fox's spin. If you don't read another book on customer service, you've got to read this one."

Jack R. Delperdang, Director of
Customer Service Oldcastle Materials

• • • • •

"J. Fox has wittily delivered a serious warning that complacency is as dangerous to your business as bad service. First place is temporary. Taking the lessons of this little book to heart will extend your run."

Deborah S. Adams, Partner,
Frost Brown Todd LLC

• • • • •

"Long term success requires an enthusiastic implementation of customer service. This unforgettable story will motivate you to charge on, and out perform your competition."

John R. Arend, Chairman of the
Board & Founder Inter-Chem

The Fable Table

Foreword by Barbara Glanz 9

Chapter 1   Scrolls and Tolls. 11

Chapter 2   The Village Report. 15

Chapter 3   Knightly Solutions 19

Chapter 4   Beyond Words 23

Chapter 5   Doogon's Deal 27

Chapter 6   Counting on the Solution 33

Chapter 7   The Message 37

Chapter 8   Inspired Journey. 41

Chapter 9   Fool Me 45

Chapter 10   Listen Up 51

Chapter 11   A Chance at Survival 55

Chapter 12   Persevere 63

Chapter 13   Inside Out. 69

Chapter 14   The Beat Goes On 75

Chapter 15   Feeling Served 81

The Scribe's Discussion Guide 88

Now, What Do You Do? 94

Want More? 95

About the Author 96

Foreword

I have worked in "customer service" for most of my life – as a daughter, a student, a teacher, a wife, a mother, a grandmother, a professional speaker, an author, and even as a friend. What I have learned over the years is that we are ALL in this world to serve one another, whatever our "work" may be. Life is all about relationships!

In this delightful, inspiring parable about the kingdom of Celelot, Joan has captured the essence of what it takes to create an organization which is based on serving – both internally and externally. The story is simple because the principles are simple. Like the king, it is only our lack of vision and our focus on the "business" part of our organization that gets in the way!

For so long, the emphasis on systems, processes, re-engineering and quality has kept us from focusing on people and relationships in our work. Of course, we must have a quality product to survive; however, in today's world, that is no longer enough. So, thank you, Joan, for so powerfully opening our eyes to the importance of the *human* level in serving others.

This story will make you smile, but it will also challenge you to examine your own "kingdom," wherever that may be, to determine how well <u>you</u> are serving <u>your</u> customers. Your "Sir Vival" will depend on it!

Blessings,

Barbara A. Glanz, Author of *CARE Packages for Your Customers – An Idea a Week to Enhance Customer Service, Building Customer Loyalty – How YOU Can Help Keep Customers Returning*, and co-author with Ken Blanchard of *The Simple Truths of Service As Inspired by Johnny the Bagger*.

CHAPTER 1

SCROLLS AND TOLLS

Once upon a time, King Steward III and Queen Jennifer reigned over the medieval Village of Celelot. They lived in the Castle and had enjoyed governing Celelot from there for more than twenty years. This village was special to them. It was where they began their married life and they earnestly wanted for it to be the best town in all the land.

For many years Celelot prospered. Favorable weather had produced an abundance of excellent crops that were known far and wide for their taste and size. The prosperity that followed ignited a surge of innovation, and improvements of all sorts were popping up everywhere.

One of the more industrious agricultural employees of Celelot discovered that feeding geese a special diet of clover and timothy grass resulted in an irresistible goose paté. An employee in the Berry Research Division of the Village added hot peppers to jam and created a blazingly sweet concoction he called "Berry Fire Jam." People flocked from all over to buy the ingenious products and boast to their neighbors about their superior purchases. Celelot had become famous for being progressive and it enjoyed the reputation, bounty and responsibility of being a premier commerce center.

The Castle provided all goods and services to the villagers and to do this it employed a vast array of specialists. Cobblers, parchment makers, weavers, carpenters, drawbridge attendants and many others worked daily to serve the villagers in Celelot, who were their customers. However, recently, there had been an upsurge of unrest in the village, and a lot of growing tension between the townspeople and the Castle.

Scrolls with complaints about Celelot had been rare when the King and Queen began their reign, but were becoming disturbingly commonplace. One scroll told of a weaver who would not exchange a moth-eaten blanket for a new one, even though the original transaction was only hours old. Additionally, complaints of the drawbridge attendants sleeping on duty and displaying a surly attitude were plentiful. The town lookouts were a source of contempt as well, always looking down on the villagers.

Yet these were not the only sources of discontent in Celelot. Lately, tolls were assigned to nearly everything, from drawing water from the village wells to crossing a footbridge. The price of living in Celelot was rising as the value of the service was falling.

And silly rules were becoming ridiculously numerous. There was a rule for this and a rule for that. There was a jest that upon awakening in the morning one had already broken two rules—waking up without permission and breathing the King's air.

The village was becoming a spoiled stew. It was seasoned with a spoonful of disappointment, a cup of frustration and a quart of disenchantment. Unbeknownst to the King and Queen, it was about to boil over.

CHAPTER 2

THE VILLAGE REPORT

At first the King and Queen turned their heads from the signs of discontent in their village. The Nobility that managed the staff gave reports of the situation at Castle meetings. At times, they even suggested solutions, but it didn't seem so bad as to warrant real concern. After all, people from the farthest reaches of the kingdom still came to Celelot to enjoy the luscious fruits, poultry innovations, Berry Fire Jam and the designer goose paté.

Late one morning as the King and Queen slept, they were startled by a hearty knock on their chamber door. The King opened the large, creaky, wooden door to a small, rather sweaty fellow who appeared before him. He panted as he explained that he had just jogged through the village, climbed the hillside, and sprinted over the drawbridge to give the King an urgent report. Still winded, he reached into his robe for his ledger and into his breast pocket for his ever-present quill, as he was the Census Taker.

"Your Majesties," he wheezed, "I have come with news

that requires your immediate notice. I have just finished the census and I have discovered a matter that is of great concern. For the first time in the history of our great village, the population is down by more than one hundred and fifty."

"Get to it then, Census Taker. Inform me of the reasons for these departures," demanded the King, rubbing his eyes and drawing his royal dressing gown closed.

Regaining his breath, the Census Taker continued. "As you know, Your Majesty, the villagers have been complaining, some even to the point of submitting scrolls about their encounters. We have known about ill-treatment from the parchment makers, the drawbridge attendants, the lookouts and many others. They also find fault with the many rules and numerous tolls which add to these sore points."

"Surely there is more to this," the King replied.

"Yes, Sire, there is. I have been told that there are nearby towns where the villagers and the Castle get along very well. Some of these towns are offering the citizens of Celelot ten geese, ten pheasants and a fortnight of free accommodations to move to their town."

"They will be back when the geese and pheasants run out," interjected the Queen. "We are still one of the largest villages around, and a few disenchanted peasants who desire pheasants should not cause us to fret. Let's forget this foolishness and speak of more important matters. We have a feast to plan for the Centennial Celebration of Celelot. And, we are in search of an artist to sculpt a likeness of our excellent King for the new fountain in the village and the search is tedious. These are the things we should be worried about."

"Respectfully, Your Majesty, one hundred and fifty-three villagers is quite a lot of our town," the Census Taker insisted. "I have run the numerals, my King, and if we lose more villagers, our commerce will surely suffer."

"Indeed, you have convinced me this is a matter of significance," replied the King turning from the Census Taker.

"My stunning Queen, I have made a decision," the King said firmly. "This defection must be stopped. Tend to the Centennial Celebration and sculpture as you will, but be advised that our first responsibility is to this concern. If we do not succeed in stopping our villagers from leaving, there will be no more anniversary celebrations, as Celelot will be but a fable!"

That night as the King lay his head on his pillow, he murmured over and over again, *What shall we do?* As he nodded off into an uneasy slumber, the King thought, *I shall summon a meeting of the Knights.*

CHAPTER 3

KNIGHTLY SOLUTIONS

"We have been commissioned by our beloved King and Queen to resolve the issue of our departing villagers," began the senior Knight, distractedly rubbing his shin with one hand. "I really wish this table were round," he added, "I keep hitting my leg against it."

"Anyway, our wise King has appointed a Scribe who will stay close to our quest and document our progress. Our Scribe, Simon, being our town crier by previous assignment, is uniquely suited for this endeavor. Let us begin.

"Simon, do record our path completely, accurately and candidly."

"This is so very simple," began the youngest of the Knights, "and not worthy of this gathering of some of the most splendid resources of the Castle. We just need to tell our villagers that we love them and ask them to stay."

"Brilliant idea," added the second youngest of the Knights. "We will make it sound pretty and post it all over town. Everyone wants to be told they are appreciated. Our post could say something like: "The villager is King.""

"Blasphemy!" retorted the senior Knight. "The King is the King. The villagers aren't Kings. I don't get your meaning."

"I've got it. I've got it," interjected the youngest Knight excitedly. "The villager is always right." Or "We try harder for our villagers." Or "Our villagers are number one."

More and more ideas were born as the meeting proceeded. But the Knights knew without a doubt that the post of words expressing their true feelings would surely keep the villagers in Celelot. After all, it was true. No one before had ever told the villagers they were special. This indeed was the answer. There was a buzz in the hall as the Knights creatively discussed how their intention should sound. So throughout the evening, after several pails of berry wine, the conclave claimed success. They had settled on the post.

They were excited. They were sure. The post would read:

EVERY DAY IS VILLAGER DAY IN CELELOT

The Scribe's Journal

This indeed is an excellent assignment—~~it pays much more than the town crier gig. After pails of berry wine~~ To resolve the problem of our villagers leaving Celelot, it has been decided by the Knights to express our appreciation for them, as this has never been done before. It is agreed that the villagers are leaving because they are feeling unappreciated. ~~Would you like some cheese with that whine? Boo-Hoo!~~ Posts will be placed throughout Celelot displaying the words "Every Day is Villager Day in Celelot."

CHAPTER 4

BEYOND WORDS

There was curiosity everywhere as the team of postmen hurried throughout the Village of Celelot attaching the posts to every flat surface. The Knights had decided to cover and seal the boards to hide the words until the unveiling. Several mischievous children attempting to remove the coating from the posts were caught, flogged lightly, and sent home to their parents.

The energy in the town bubbled higher and higher as people passed on rumors and spun wild tales about the mysterious message on the posts. There were reports of the King and Queen sharing their significant profits with the villagers. Other reports told of a day where everything in Celelot would be free to all villagers.

A marvelous mood had overtaken Celelot. The unveiling was to take place at a special town celebration.

On the day of the celebration, merry men danced, jesters performed, and the Village Orator spoke lofty words. The Castle even planned a jousting match for the entertainment of the villagers.

When the trumpets sounded, the King and Queen, adorned in robes of ruby and gold (they enjoyed dressing alike) floated into the gathering. The Knights swiftly took their places flanking the posts, ready at the signal from the King to reveal their content.

"My dear villagers," began the King. "As we approach the Centennial of our beloved Celelot, I deem it fitting to bestow upon you something not experienced by any villager until this moment. As you know, of late, some of your fellow villagers have left our swell town for other places. We in the Castle have spent many days and nights trying to figure out why. And I am proud to tell you, we think we now know. Everyone wants to be told they are appreciated. So my dear souls, I am happy to give you this long overdue gift."

Excited voices raised from the crowd as every villager anticipated the message on the posts. The King gave the signal and with one swipe of each Knight's sword the cover was removed from each post. The people gasped with excitement, anticipating the words on the post. There they were, exposed for all to see.

Silence befell the crowd.

"Look! They are speechless!" remarked the Queen as she excitedly clapped her hands. "They are absolutely speechless."

The King, visibly happy with himself, spoke again. "I see you are in awe of these fine words. And indeed they are sincere. We appreciate you. So let us continue this grand celebration until the sun bids farewell for the day."

The Scribe's Journal

And yet another exciting event to report! I regret that this entry may be my last, as success has come quickly. ~~Darn it--Cake jobs like this are hard to find.~~ Upon unveiling the posts of appreciation at a grand village festival, the villagers were speechless. This appears to have been the problem all along—that our villagers felt unappreciated. ~~Who knew? The end.~~

CHAPTER 5

DOOGON'S DEAL

In the Castle the next morning, the King and Queen and all of the Nobility were feeling proud. There was a kind of release, a kind of virtue in finally telling the villagers that they were appreciated. It was freeing, in a way. One could get the attitude that the villagers weren't essential. Some had never considered that without villagers Celelot would not be. Celelot had thrived because the villagers used the goods and services of the Castle. But many of the Nobility had felt indifferent to the villagers and their complaints most of their lives. It seemed that life would be pretty good without them, especially since they could be a complaining sort.

In the town that very morning, the feeling couldn't have been more opposite. The villagers were disappointed. They couldn't believe that after all the build-up, the only thing they got was "Every Day is Villager Day in Celelot." What happened to the real things? How did rumors of profit sharing and "free day" get started?

"What a load of goose feathers," exclaimed the villager, John, to his friend Harry. "I have never witnessed such silly goings on. The King and Queen have been misled if there is a chance they believe 'Every Day is Villager Day in Celelot' changes our lives. They puffed their chests up like proud roosters. Cock a Doodle Doo! Who could have foreseen such a foolish thing as this?"

"Yes," laughed Harry. "They must have consumed quite a quantity of berry wine to have contrived such an absurd scheme. This post of words does not turn Celelot into Camelot."

As the men were conversing, a noblewoman strolled by. "I couldn't help but overhear your words just now," she said. "I must say I am troubled by what I've heard the two of you express. Did we not please you with our words?"

"Milady," began John. "I do not wish to cause trouble. We were merely jesting."

But the noblewoman pressed on. "I beg you to tell me the truth, sirs. Even though I am disappointed in what I hear, I earnestly seek understanding."

John spoke first. "Milady, here is why the villagers feel let down. Great expectations were married to the post of words prior to the unveiling. But when the cloth came off, and your meanings were revealed, they were just words. After years of being ignored, forgotten, and even taken advantage of, we villagers expected more than words. Words are too easily spoken."

"Words are too easily spoken," repeated the noblewoman as she let the meaning simmer for a moment. "I thank you two gentle men for your candor. I will see that your thoughts land on the ears of the King."

The noblewoman quickly returned to the Castle and relayed the conversation she heard to the King and Queen who were both perplexed and disappointed upon hearing the thoughts of the two villagers.

"My King," urged the noblewoman. "I trust you will now seek a Solutionist to help us with our problem."

"Indeed this matter appears to be more complex than we first assumed," responded the King. "Quickly! Journey to the center of town, find Sir Doogon and bring him to the Castle. Before the day is done, we will have a meeting about this."

Later that day, the noblewoman and Sir Doogon arrived back at the Castle where all the Knights and the senior Nobility were gathered in anticipation.

Sir Doogon was a polite and refined man. He was shaven and bathed nearly daily. When he glided into the chamber, his stylish pantaloons made a swishing sound, causing the attendees to note his entrance. He was a competitive swordsman and his muscles protruding gently from his shirt commanded respect. He spoke of "data points," "high-level discussions," and "addition by subtraction." He expressed that something was "mission critical" and suggested a "roadmap of highly designed deliverables." These phrases impressed the King, Queen and Nobility.

"Let's get to it," declared the King. "Sir Doogon, Celelot is losing villagers. We look to you for recommendations."

"Not to worry, my dear friends. Let us not bother with those villagers. We can get new ones," stated Sir Doogon confidently. "Celelot is a fine town. We need to beckon others from neighboring towns to come here. So even though our villagers are leaving, we can offer reduced tolls, pheasants and geese for newcomers' allegiance to Celelot. This is easy. Trust me. This technique is a classic repair for difficulties of such sort. Villagers will flock to us when they hear of our generous offer."

So the very next day messengers rode with public notices to neighboring towns. The notices boldly stated the offer from Celelot.

Indeed villagers from other towns did respond and before long many came to live in the town of Celelot.

The Scribe's Journal

The posts of appreciation did not make a difference so we hired the fine Solutionist, Sir Doogon, who recommended that we increase our village population by offering incentives to villagers from other towns. This indeed was successful in getting new villagers to come to Celelot. Unfamiliar faces are becoming familiar. ~~HA HA! We did it. Hurrah!!~~ We found our solution. The Village of Celelot flourishes once again! This may be the end. So I am signing off.

Simon, the Scribe

CHAPTER 6

COUNTING ON THE SOLUTION

The King, keenly aware of the many new faces in the village, was anxious to declare success over the problem of the declining village population.

"My lovely Queen, I am eager to understand how much we are growing. As far as we know, Celelot could well be Swell-a-lot," he laughed. "We have been using Sir Doogon's solution for three months now. Life is fine. Let's summon the Census Taker and see how fine it is."

Although not thrilled by the request to once again go door to creaking door and count heads, the Census Taker agreed nonetheless. After all, who could say "no" to the King?

Near the completion of his task, on the very edge of the village on the way out of town was a dwelling owned by the Tarot reader, Pearl. She insisted that he stay for a spot of tea. Exhausted from this latest undertaking of many days, he agreed. Pearl glanced at the Census Taker's ledger.

"You will be surprised when your tally is complete," stated Pearl. "You are expecting a rebirth in our town but really the town is shrinking in size, not growing. I know this because I have a special gift for these things."

Just then several Celelotians hurried past Pearl's window. They waved to her as they passed her house. *One, two, three,* Pearl counted in her head. And with her back turned away from the Census Taker, she reached into her pocket and made several marks upon a piece of parchment.

"My gift tells me that Celelot is still declining in population," Pearl repeated to the Census Taker.

This could not be so, he thought. *The population cannot still be declining.*

The Census Taker said an abrupt "goodbye" and rode swiftly to his home where he sat up half the night, counting, recounting, checking, and double checking his tally. Greater than the disappointment in the numbers, was the fear of telling the King and Queen that Sir Doogon's solution had not worked.

Unbeknownst to the King, Queen and Census Taker, many of the townspeople were once again disappointed, some insulted. The Castle had decided to shower fine gifts upon newcomers without any consideration for the original villagers. They felt that their loyalty didn't matter as it was not being recognized or rewarded. So, as new people came because of the incentives, the original villagers left in droves.

The Scribe's Journal

I thought we had found the solution. I would have sworn to it. There were new villagers everywhere. However, the village count is down. ~~As I write this fine piece of literature~~, They continue to move to other villages. ~~I didn't think adding by subtracting sounded right! What was that about? Glad it's not my job to tell the King.~~ ~~WHEW!!~~

CHAPTER 7

THE MESSAGE

The Census Taker slept not one wink and arose from his cot with the first light of the day. A soaking rain watered the crops, quenched the hillside and drenched him on his way to the Castle. He arrived at the moat surrounding the Castle. Things were always floating in the moat waters and it occurred to him, because of the ill news that he carried, that he too may be doing some moat-floating before the day was up.

"Greetings, Census Taker," exclaimed the handmaiden excitedly as she opened the door to a very muddy, moist and melancholy man. "The mood in the Castle has been light and sure of good news today. I will escort you to the parlor where the King and Queen are having their tea."

He followed the handmaiden to what was sure to be one of his final moments on this earth. *Everyone wants to shoot the messenger,* he thought. *I hope the King has pity on this one, today.*

"Happy greetings to you," spoke the Queen, almost dancing across the floor to the Census Taker. "Let's hear this lovely news!"

The King stood up and pounded the Census Taker on the back in a hearty gesture of friendliness. The Census Taker, recovering from the pain of the blow, readied himself to speak.

"My good and reasonable King," he began, "I bring news that will not fall easily on your ears. I will be forthright and get to it quickly. I will tell you this right now so you don't have to wonder about the state of your village. As soon as I can get the words to part my lips, you will know what I know."

"Good sir, get on with it," urged the King.

"Sire, the village count is down. I know I have disappointed you, kind sir, and stand ready for my punishment," stammered the Census Taker.

"What sort of moron would shoot the messenger?" questioned the King. "Be aware that your words disappoint me greatly. But I believe you have shown great courage today. Anyway, my darling Queen, have Castle Security escort him to his horse, take his Castle pass and tell him he no longer is welcomed here in Celelot."

The Census Taker sadly looked down at the floor.

"Ha, ha, ha," laughed the King, "I merely jest. I apologize for my feeble attempt to make light of this matter as I desperately yearn for some relief. But truly this trouble gets graver. This once little problem has grown out of hand. We now not only have a diminishing village, but even those who are loyal to us are upset with us right now."

That night the King was extremely worried. Previously there had been hope. Since nothing had been tried, nothing had failed. He sat on his throne most of the night hoping to derive some kind of wisdom from all the great Kings who had sat on it before him. He did not want to be the King who started his reign with a prosperous kingdom and ended it in disaster.

The King thought all night until his royal head hurt. Thoroughly exhausted, he fell into a deep slumber and began dreaming about his youth. They were certainly better days than these. His old friends Otto and Vival appeared before him. Otto was now the King of Sellmoor and Vival – now Sir Vival, was a retired Solutionist who still lived in Celelot.

Captured by the land of dreams, the King's elbow slipped from the arm of the throne and he caught himself before hitting the floor. His crown crashed to the ground with a resounding echo. As he watched it wobble back and forth on the floor, an inspiration hit him.

The Scribe's Journal

Our Census Taker has once again delivered news of a dwindling population to the King and Queen. Things are worse. ~~This stinks (just kidding)~~ ~~just really glad I'm not the Census Taker.~~ ☺

CHAPTER 8

INSPIRED JOURNEY

The journey was one that only the King himself could make. Inspired by his dream the evening before, he mounted his sturdy steed and traveled to a remote part of Celelot, where his old friend Sir Vival lived.

Sir Vival was a retired Solutionist who only withdrew from his private affairs for matters of great significance. Most of his time was spent in contemplation in his garden. He loved putting his hands in the rich brown soil of Celelot and feeling its soft, moist texture. Because of the care he gave to the garden he loved, it loved him back with abundance and beauty. The array of colors and the varieties of flowers were unmatched anywhere in the land. The fruits and vegetables were succulent and their sweet juices dripped freely when bitten.

"Sir Vival," shouted the King excitedly as he approached his ally in the midst of his thriving tomato vines. "I awoke this morning with you on my mind and traveled the day to see you. How are you?"

"My King, I am delighted to see you. How long has it been since we have spoken?"

"Far too long, my dear friend," responded the King.

"I desire to know what brings you to this remote part of Celelot today. Let us go inside and have some berry wine and you can tell me what is on your mind."

"That is a fine idea," agreed the King.

As they ambled into the simple dwelling, the King removed his crown and took a seat. Sir Vival poured the wine as the King began. "I have worries of the greatest sort on my mind," he said.

As the evening went on, the King and Sir Vival discussed the matter of the declining village population at length. The conversation lasted well into the night and the King, weary from his journey, spent the night with his good friend, Sir Vival. It was exactly the retreat he needed to gather his thoughts and escape for a few moments from what seemed like impending failure.

In the morning, the two mounted their horses and rode at an urgent pace toward the center of town. The King felt confident and hopeful with his friend by his side. Sir Vival, filled with a desire to serve his King, felt determined and enthusiastic about the adventure before him.

He loved a good challenge and indeed this challenge was good. He quickly thought of his old friend Sophie, whom he knew he could count on to support his new mission. And with every stride of his horse, he felt his passion for the quest mounting.

Immediately upon his arrival at the Castle, Sir Vival was escorted to a special feast celebrating his arrival. The culinary staff prepared pheasant with orange glacé, soured dough cherry rolls, sugared yams, roasted squash, wild mushrooms and the standard assortment of dried fruits and nuts. In addition to the magnificent food, the room was filled with opinions, most of which were not complimentary to the King's decision.

"How absurd is this new twist," stated Leo, the Master of Arms. He was respected and admired for having defeated every contender for his title. "It is bizarre to believe that a retired codger who is an old friend of the King can out-think the real Solutionist we hired to fix this very issue."

"It does appear to be a mistake," responded Keeg, Celelot's specialist in charge of complex calculations. "It is necessary that we address our problem with an effective solution, as I have determined that every day our problem continues, the GKP (Gross Kingdom Product) declines. This I predict will cause Celelot to lose Kingdom status in three months."

Similar conversations developed throughout the room. The mood was pessimistic and doubts were everywhere.

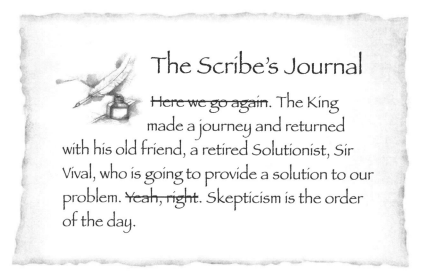

The Scribe's Journal

~~Here we go again.~~ The King made a journey and returned with his old friend, a retired Solutionist, Sir Vival, who is going to provide a solution to our problem. ~~Yeah, right.~~ Skepticism is the order of the day.

CHAPTER 9

FOOL ME

It had been years since Sir Vival had been anywhere close to the Castle. As he breathed in the lavender and berry-filled air, a rejuvenated feeling came over him. The fragrant breeze reminded him of a time years ago when he lived in a simple hut just steps from the Castle moat and among some of the village's most interesting inhabitants.

And now, he was on a mission to find one of them – his wise, old friend Sophie. These days, however, she was wrongly thought of as the town fool. Sir Vival was told that Sophie lived by the huge oak tree that stood next to the wide, rushing stream on the west side of the Castle.

"Sophie! Sophie!" called Sir Vival as he approached the big oak next to the stream. "This is Sir Vival. Where are you?"

"Look up, Sir Vival. Look up," responded Sophie.

Sir Vival looked up and gazed on a face brimming with delight at his arrival. Sophie had constructed a living space from canvas and planks. It appeared to be quite sturdy and supported her meager furnishings. Fresh flowers in colorful pots adorned the space, and gave clues to the owner's temperament.

"I am perplexed," shouted Sir Vival as he cast his eyes upwards. "Why are you living in a tree?"

"Simple," responded Sophie. "It makes me smarter. Up here I see things no one else can see. I know what I know because I see what I see."

"My visit has an important purpose, Sophie. Our good King has enlisted me to remedy our town's declining population. Feeling duty to my King and love for my village, I have agreed to help. So, I have come to receive your wisdom."

Sophie responded, "Wisdom is not received, Sir Vival; it is discovered. So let us go on this adventure together."

With an enthusiastic nod from Sir Vival, Sophie continued.

"The solutions that were proposed before were artificial ones. They were based on nothing. Let us focus first on the posts. Yes, everyone wants to be appreciated, but you can't just tell villagers after years of indifference that you appreciate them. There is no reason to believe it; no foundation for the words to lie on; no history that would make them true," Sophie said as her voice became increasing excited. "There were no changes in behavior toward the villagers. 'Everyday is Villager Day in Celelot' was hollow.

"The next solution was to offer pheasants and geese to people in other villages to bribe them to come to Celelot. Tell me, my friend, for what reasons do you believe this solution failed?"

"Well," Sir Vival responded, "I have seen this misdirected solution many times. It did get the attention of villagers from other towns, but those living in Celelot felt cast aside. After all, they had spent their entire lives in Celelot and now perfect strangers were being treated better than they were. They felt more than disappointed, perhaps betrayed.

"For some this would sound like an excellent solution, but long term it does not work," continued Sir Vival as he shook his head back and forth. "The loyal villagers were now being treated like second-class citizens. All the attention was on bringing new-comers into the town. Celelot forgot."

Sophie paused and then repeated the phrase. "Celelot forgot. That rhymes," she giggled.

Sir Vival affirmed, "We forgot that we must care for our loyal villagers at least in the same ways we care for new villagers who come to our town."

"It is amazing that many villages use this 'fill the leaking pail' idea," stated Sophie. "This is short-term thinking, for sure. Getting new villagers is always more enticing than keeping the ones you have. And indeed it is important to get new ones, but it must be *balanced* with efforts to keep the current villagers.

"Ask Keeg how much it cost us for the pheasants and geese and all. It was a King's fortune! Spending to attract new villagers somehow seems justified—because there is a temporary swell in the village, but the truth is that our loyal villagers should be rewarded in some way too. Otherwise, it is a silly game we play as villages keep exchanging villagers."

"Sophie, I learned from you years ago that how we behave is critically affected by how we feel. We feel and then we act. This explains a lot. The villagers of Celelot did not feel valued and therefore they left. They did not feel served.

"We must remind ourselves that **there is a difference between getting served and feeling served**," continued Sir Vival. "Anyone can grant a request and serve a villager. But the villager only *feels* served when the request is granted with a willing heart.

"If a villager requests a goose to be plucked clean of its feathers, a butcher could pluck the goose, toss the goose to the villager and then rudely demand payment. The villager would get what he asked for, a plucked goose. He would get served. But the villager would not *feel* served.

"Or that same butcher could greet the villager as he would his best friend, engage in a bit of a conversation, cheerfully pluck the goose, ask if he needed anything else, and warmly invite the villager to visit him again. Of course, the goose would be plucked totally clean. And the villager would leave feeling served.

"There are three things that need to happen for the villager to feel served and therefore choose to stay here in Celelot."

Throughout the remainder of the day, Sir Vival and his wise friend explored possibilities, philosophies and theories. They challenged each other in a way that may have led any passerby to believe that they were arguing. But they were not. They were thinking.

Because they were open, new thoughts flowed like the rushing stream that sang under them. At the end of their long discussion, there was even more than new hope: they had a plan.

They discovered three things that needed to happen for the villagers to *feel* served and therefore choose to stay in Celelot.

The Scribe's Journal

Our new Solutionist, Sir Vival, found his old friend, Sophie, in a tree today. ~~This just keeps getting weirder.~~ He tells me she is wise. ~~But she does live in a tree.~~ Sophie and Sir Vival examined the previous solutions and discussed why they failed. They now have a new plan to keep our villagers in Celelot by making them "feel served." ~~And I've got some land I would like to sell you in Camelot. I'm keeping my fingers crossed.~~

WINNING ...
The First Merchants Way

CHAPTER 10

LISTEN UP

With a sense of urgency, Sir Vival left Sophie and set out for the Castle. He arrived just in time for the pre-arranged meeting with the King, Queen and Nobility. The mood in the air was negative. The optimism that prevailed under leadership of Sir Doogon was glaringly absent. Whining about the situation of the declining village population had replaced any real activity, strategy or constructive thinking about the problem.

Sir Vival stood at the front of the parlor to address the disapproving attendees. He began in a non-spirited tone and described in detail why the previous attempts to keep the villagers in Celelot had failed. Heads began to nod one by one. He asserted that the first thing the assembly needed to do was to harness enough energy to be hopeful again.

"Of course a hopeful spirit is far from enough to save our village," explained Sir Vival. "Hence, I wish to discuss with you what else we must do to create a thriving Celelot once again. We must make our villagers feel good about, even proud of being citizens of Celelot."

Sir Vival paused for a moment then said, "We must make them feel served here in Celelot. When we accomplish this, our villagers will be loyal to us and Celelot will flourish once again.

"We looked at our crisis in a gallant way, indeed," he continued. "We sought solutions zealously. But the key to unlocking the mystery of why our villagers are leaving has thus far eluded us. Today we begin a new path with a new goal. Our goal is to make our villagers *feel* served. And the first step on that journey is to listen to them and act upon what we hear. For years we dismissed the complaints and chose not to hear the stories of woe until now when we cannot turn our ears away any longer. So today we change this and we listen."

Sir Vival outlined a strategy to listen to the villagers and launched the plan immediately. Parchments with complaints that had piled up over the years were analyzed. Teams went out into the village in an organized fashion to listen to the people of Celelot.

The information was compiled and, indeed, most of the news was dreadful. However, there were also some promising reports. The villagers spoke highly of their dealings with every aspect of the Agriculture Department. This was the one bright spot, a solitary star, in an otherwise dark sky.

"My King, it seems there is a single segment of our village that is performing exceptionally well in our villagers eyes," stated Sir Vival. "I am eager to learn the reasons the Agriculture Department is perceived to be superior. Do you have any opinions as to why this is so?"

"The Agriculture Department is privileged to sell our finest product. Buyers come from far away to purchase the fruits and vegetable grown in our soil. This could be the reason," replied the King.

"You make a decent point, my noble King," responded Sir Vival, "but is it not so that our weavers have won multiple awards over the most recent years for the quality of their goods? And that our parchment makers have participated

in the festivals, returning home victorious for their works? If indeed the quality of the produce was the cause of this satisfaction, would not our villagers sing the praises of our weavers and our parchment makers too? I believe we may have discovered the holders of the secret."

The Scribe's Journal

We had yet another meeting about our ~~miserable~~ villagers leaving. In general, everyone is fatigued by this problem. Sir Vival's "solution" was to "listen" to our villagers. So we sent teams out to "listen" to the villagers and found out that the villagers were mostly unhappy. ~~DUH~~! However, they gave the Agriculture Department positive marks. ~~Finally, some good news~~.

CHAPTER 11

A CHANCE AT SURVIVAL

Sir Vival sprinted out the door, his mind set upon discovering the reasons behind the Agriculture Department's success. Upon arriving, he approached a small structure with bins lined with colorfully dyed burlap. In them lay the most fabulous fruits and vegetables one could imagine. The vibrant hues created a tempting and edible rainbow.

Tapping a woman on the shoulder, Sir Vival asked, "Do you know where I can find the noble in charge of this department?"

"Yes, I do," spoke the woman as she turned and flashed a bright smile toward her inquisitor. "I am Rose, the noblewoman in charge. I am here to serve you, Sir. How may I be of help?"

Thrust an arrow into my heart, thought Sir Vival as he struggled to begin his next thought. *This Rose is surely rare.*

"An apt name indeed," he responded. "Good morning, Fair Rose. I am Sir Vival and I am visiting to understand how it is that your department is the only one in all of Celelot that the villagers desire to do business with. May we spend some time together so I may understand how this is so?"

"Certainly, Sir Vival. I would be delighted. I love Celelot and if there is anything that my department can do to increase our chance of survival, I am happy to help. Let me show you around," Rose replied.

As Rose and Sir Vival toured the Agriculture Department, many villagers stopped to speak to Rose. She greeted them happily, answering their questions. She recommended the best parsnips for stew and the most succulent apples for tarts and then took them to the goods they were seeking. She also spoke to the employees and assisted them with villagers. It was an illuminating tour for Sir Vival; one where he became aware of the clear priority in Rose's mind: The villager came first.

Sir Vival spent the day with Rose and then returned the next morning. As he strolled through the Agriculture Department, he noted the upbeat way the employees related to the villagers. Without exception, they welcomed the customers warmly and genuinely. And, after inquiring about their needs, they quickly fulfilled them while engaging in a bit of pleasant conversation.

These workers greet the townspeople as if they actually care about them, thought Sir Vival. *And they carry out requests as if they were urgent.*

On more than one occasion Sir Vival noticed that a villager was about to purchase some goods which had unnoticed damage. The clerk pointed it out and then proceeded to select better quality for the patron. Without exception, the villagers expressed delight.

They are really looking out for the villager's best interest, thought Sir Vival.

A time or two, a couple of people requested goods that were currently unavailable. The employee informed the villagers that she would send notice as soon as the goods arrived.

That is exceptional service, thought Sir Vival. *The employee did not request that the villager check back with her, but she took the responsibility to alert the individual when the goods would be available.*

There was one occasion when a woman was upset, as she had experienced multiple problems and took her anger out on the employee. The employee listened to the villager and, after a few moments, apologized sincerely for the frustration she had experienced. She then asked questions and recorded the responses on parchment. The employee resolved the situation without even consulting Rose. The woman thanked the employee and left placated, with a smile on her satisfied face.

That was handled well, thought Sir Vival. *The employee turned the entire situation around. If she hadn't been so skilled, the problem could have spiraled out of control. But instead, the villager left quite pleased and filled with gratitude.*

Further conversations with Rose revealed even more behind why the Agriculture Department was so deeply loved. The most intriguing reason being that she only hired "happy" people.

"Happy is as important as knowledgeable. I don't believe that I can *teach* people to be positive and come to work everyday with a great attitude," she told Sir Vival. "And because most everything we do in our department involves relating to our villagers in some way, this is very important. Besides, even those tasks that don't involve face-to-face time with villagers, do involve face-to-face time with others in our department. I cannot have someone complaining all the time. It affects us inside the department and eventually, our villagers would be affected too."

"This indeed is true," replied Sir Vival. "It is one of the common sense rules of villager service that most ignore."

Rose also spoke about the Department's "Villager Service" reputation. She gave her employees compliments when they handled villagers with a smile and a solution. And the employees praised each other, too.

Each employee put his or her own special touch on how

they interacted with villagers, like a fingerprint. One employee used the phrase "excellent choice" in an enthusiastic voice with each villager selection. Another employee posted his suggestions daily. Today, he posted five selections for Berry Fire Jam pairings. Every single employee in the Agriculture Department was proud to be there—and the villagers knew it.

Sir Vival thanked Rose and went to work using her department as a model. All the other departments in Celelot were instructed in their ways, the best ways, of relating to the villager.

Sir Vival focused on four themes:

1 – Make the villager feel important
- Genuinely welcome the villager
- Listen attentively to the villager
- Be responsive to their needs
- Thank them for their business

2 – Demonstrate that you have the villager's best interest in mind
- Be knowledgeable in your job
- Think about what the villager needs before they know they need it
- Make sure that what the villager selects is unflawed and the best fit for their needs

3 – Welcome villager complaints

- Listen attentively to the upset villager
- Apologize sincerely
- Respond respectfully, empathically and non-defensively
- Own the situation and correct it with a sense of urgency

4 – Put your fingerprint on your villager service

- Put "you" into your service. Just as your fingerprint is uniquely yours, so is your style of service. This makes the villager's experience memorable.

The lessons to the employees and the nobles were delivered with enthusiasm and received like parched ground welcomes the rain. It was at once apparent that Celelot was undergoing a metamorphosis. All of the departments in Celelot were trying their very best to follow in the footsteps of the Agriculture Department.

After a period of time, the official team of listeners went out into the village to see if the changes had improved villager satisfaction. Indeed the news was good. The villagers appeared to be much happier with Celelot. Elated, the King, Queen, and Nobility began a flurry of activity in preparation for a town festival. Sir Vival immediately declared that it was too soon and recommended that the Census Taker be called upon once again to assess the village population.

The Scribe's Journal

Sir Vival used the Agriculture Department as a model to learn from and to instruct the other departments. Celelot has made many changes. Even I had to go through training. There is news that the villagers are more satisfied. The King wants to have a festival to celebrate success. Sir Vival wishes to take another census. I wish to go to the festival.

CHAPTER 12

PERSEVERE

The King was reluctant to summon the Census Taker. There was real evidence that the mood in Celelot was much better and the villagers were satisfied. The village spent much effort to get the villagers to stay and it seemed like the time to celebrate, not beat a dead mule.

"My King," began Sir Vival, "I agree it has been a long and difficult path. And it appears that the problem has been resolved. However, we have only taken the first step on our journey to making our villagers feel served. We listened to the villagers and acted upon what we discovered. All the departments have been instructed in the best ways to interact with our villagers. Indeed this is an important step, but may I remind you, it is only the first. Let us count villagers once again to make sure our efforts have made us some progress."

"Sir Vival," replied the King, "I am not certain if it is your plain logic or the fact that I am weary that compels me to listen to you again. I will stay the course and let you fatigue my poor Census Taker once more."

So the Census Taker once again went from door to creaking door to count villagers. By this time he had become a familiar face and the villagers were pleased to see him. They invited him in for tea, and in some cases, berry wine.

When he reached the edge of town and Pearl's home, she asked him to come inside to compare numbers. The Census Taker had not yet counted his markings but was convinced that the result would be good.

"I disagree with you," said Pearl. "My gift allows me to know things that most cannot know. Once you count the marks on your ledger, you will be aware that the town of Celelot is still diminishing. The rate of villagers leaving is not as great as before, but Celelot is still shrinking."

Since Pearl had been accurate in the past, the Census Taker's mood became desperate. He had only one thought. This time the unfortunate messenger, knowing the King's patience was wearing thin, would surely suffer some sort of ill fate.

So the downtrodden Census Taker added up his markings and discovered that Pearl was definitely right again. The population was still declining. The only good news was that it wasn't disappearing at the rate it had been before. *But that is really good news,* the Census Taker thought. Almost immediately, his mood changed. *I will begin with this when I approach my King.*

Really, the Census Taker thought as he tried hard to convince himself and muster up his courage to inform the King. *Really. It's good news. It could be worse...I think.*

As he crossed the moat, he again envisioned himself floating in the water amidst the animal carcasses. He quickly dismissed the thought and rushed into the Castle where he was met by the Queen.

"My beautiful Queen, I have journeyed now three times in the service of Your Majesty and my King. I, more than anyone, want to please you," spoke the Census Taker. "However, I fear, rather I know, that I will once again disappoint you. So, I will get to it."

"You do not need to tell me more," said the Queen. "Your demeanor speaks for you. It is obvious that we failed."

"Failed would be a strong word," said Sir Vival entering the room. "We have started on a journey that is not easy. We started a process and have only completed the first step. Let us keep to it."

"Where is the King?" asked the Census Taker.

"He is on the throne," replied the Queen as she winked. "He will be here in a moment or two or three."

Just then the King arrived. Seeing the Census Taker and

Sir Vival, he vigorously slapped them on their backs. After recovering, they stood straight and told him the news.

"For the love of my mother," said the King. "Is there no solution to our problem? This cannot be so! I beg you, bring me better news. This has been a challenging path and you tell me our progress is so small as to be almost non-existent!"

"Yes, my dear King," said the Queen. "But do not despair. This news is disappointing yet there are signs that we are advancing in the right direction. Our loyal Census Taker informed me that there are villagers who were thinking of going to another town but decided to stay here. There is still hope. We have not been defeated yet."

"My kind Queen," whispered Sir Vival, "thank you for your support. I do know we can solve this puzzle. I do know Celelot will endure. Though we are indeed making progress, there are still two more important steps before we can be on top once again."

The Scribe's Journal

<u>The Census Taker's results:</u> We
are still losing population but the
rate of loss has slowed considerably. ~~Yippee~~!
The King and Sir Vival agree that we should
stay the course, as "listening and acting
upon the feedback" was only one step in the
process. Sir Vival said that we have just begun
to listen and that it will take time to turn this
~~beast~~ predicament around after years of
indifference.

CHAPTER 13

INSIDE OUT

More determined than ever to win back Celelot's golden reputation and halt any further exodus on the part of its residents, Sir Vival instructed the Nobility to further examine the Census Taker's ledger. The inquiry revealed that the villagers were not the only ones defecting but some of Celelot's employees had moved to other towns. It was rapidly realized that unless the best employees were happy enough to stay in Celelot and gladly provide great service to the villagers, the villagers certainly wouldn't stay.

"Sir Vival, what do you make of this new information?" asked the King. "This entire time we have been focusing on making sure that the villagers were satisfied and it is evident that our own employees feel underappreciated and discontented – some even to the point of leaving Celelot."

"You are right, my King. While we were intensely focused on listening to our villagers, we forgot to listen to our employees. So, bear with me through the duration of this solution," Sir Vival responded as he dashed toward the doorway.

Sir Vival gathered the employees of Celelot together in the village square and encouraged them to voice their concerns. The complaints were heartfelt and numerous, with the two most popular being that the Nobility constantly demanded longer working hours and that getting a break to use the privy was rare. In addition, the employees were not always kind to each other and many felt disrespected by their co-workers. In some departments there was even a feeling of distrust. In short, many employees expressed deep dissatisfaction.

Sir Vival quilled as much information as his parchment would hold and then began to write on his arms. The Kingdom had recently announced an initiative to go "parchmentless" and, being loyal, he was trying to set a good example. Satisfied that he understood the employees well, he pledged that the King would hear their concerns in their most honest form.

Arriving at the now familiar Castle parlor, Sir Vival sat for a few moments and contemplated the new information. He remembered what he and Sophie had discussed—**how people behave is critically affected by how they feel.**

He also recalled the plan that he and Sophie outlined. Step two on the path to making the villagers feel served was to make sure that the employees were satisfied. If the employees of Celelot felt dissatisfied, they probably revealed their dissatisfaction in the way they behaved toward the villagers. So, to keep the villagers in Celelot, it was critical to make changes that would improve the quality of their employment in Celelot.

Sir Vival thought, *Service begins inside out.* A good apple has a good core. So if Celelot was to survive, those on the inside, the employees, were an important part of the equation.

The Queen entered the parlor and watched as Sir Vival twisted and turned his arm and then pulled the skin tight to read his scribblings. *Poor dear,* she thought, *this man is obviously under a lot of pressure.*

"Sir Vival," she said, "I see that you have returned." As she poured him a cup of hot tea, she asked, "Was your excursion into the village a successful one?"

"Yes, quite so," he assured her. "And it is apparent that we have new opportunities for improvement. OFI's I like to call them."

What an odd choice of words, thought the Queen. *Solutionists must stay up all night, thinking of peculiar ways to say things.* For a moment she feared she might have said these words out loud, but was quickly reassured that she had not done so by the enthusiastic look on Sir Vival's face.

"Think of Celelot's employees as the energizers of the village," stated Sir Vival. "I would go so far as to say that they actually *are* Celelot to our villagers. When they are happy, they care more deeply about meeting the expectations of the villagers. Since we are in a competitive environment with other villages, quality employees are of critical importance to us. And right now our employees are not satisfied."

The King interrupted, "Oxen pies! Our employees have never expressed the discontent you speak about."

"My glorious King, we must make a serious review of our employees' concerns. There are other towns where our employees can work. All of our employees could leave and where would we be then? If it is possible to make them glad they work in Celelot, why would we resist doing this?"

"You do have a gift for persuasion, my friend. Do what needs to be done to make our employees happy," said the King.

So, by the King's command, the Nobility made the changes that would make the kingdom's employees proud to say they worked in Celelot. These changes were decided upon based on the employee interviews as well as Sir Vival's observations. Also, the employees began treating each other as they would treat the villagers. They began communicating with respect and responding to each other's needs with a smile and an earnest will to help that had been absent far too long.

The Scribe's Journal

And yet another issue has been uncovered. Upon a review of the Census Taker's notes, it was found that our beloved employees are also leaving Celelot. Sir Vival did some more of his "listening" and identified the reasons the employees are so unhappy. ~~It appears that everyone in Celelot has gone batty.~~ The village has taken great pains to address ALL the matters of concern. Sir Vival says "service begins inside out" or something like that. Supposedly our villagers will benefit from the improved relationships with the employees. ~~Let's hope so. My fingers AND toes and legs and arms are crossed.~~

CHAPTER 14

THE BEAT GOES ON

The Village of Celelot seemed in some ways like a new place. There were smiles on faces and friendly banter in the streets as the villagers shopped happily. Sir Vival, however, was cautiously optimistic. There was something still itching in the back of his mind and he felt compelled to go to Sophie once more.

He traveled to her tree by the stream and found her standing on her head, balancing her body against the tree and mumbling some kind of mantra.

Sophie saw Sir Vival approach but maintained her inverted position.

"What is the purpose of your unusual stance, my friend?" asked Sir Vival.

"It keeps my blood flowing and lubricates my brain. I do my best thinking while on my head. I already know why you are here. We need to speak some more about the third step on the path to keeping our villagers loyal to Celelot."

"Okay, you have my attention," responded Sir Vival. "Can you help?"

"We knew the third step was to build a relationship with the villager and relationships take time," Sophie replied, laboring a bit to hold a conversation in her inverted pose. "Even though the employees of Celelot are taking good care of the villagers, the villagers need to believe that things will stay this way. What we have begun must still be there tomorrow and the next day and the next."

Sir Vival nodded his agreement saying, "When the villagers experience consistent good treatment, they will be loyal to Celelot as Celelot will have proven that it deserves their loyalty."

"All of our efforts, Sir Vival, will be short-lived unless it is truly understood that building relationships is the key," said Sophie as she maneuvered herself to an upright position. "Think about the ingredients of a good relationship. There is communication, trust, respect, reliability, responsiveness and empathy. When these things are experienced over time, they become predictable."

"When the King, the Queen and the Nobility understand that their real job is to build a relationship with the villagers and with the employees based on these ingredients, the villagers and the employees will be loyal to Celelot," articulated Sophie as she moved closer to Sir Vival. "And when the employees understand that their job is to develop a relationship with the villagers, and each other, the villagers will in turn be loyal to them."

"So it is not just about villagers being satisfied, then?" queried Sir Vival.

"No, a satisfied, happy villager today can be an unhappy, dissatisfied villager tomorrow," stated Sophie. "It is about building good relationships. If an employee takes the time to develop a relationship with the villager and the villager becomes unhappy, it is highly likely that the villager will give the employee another chance *because* there is a relationship."

"This is all very nice, Sophie, but to some, this may seem soft. It may appear to be more theoretical than practical. I'm not convinced that I can travel back to the King and talk about building relationships."

"My friend, Sir Vival, let us get practical then. Let us talk about the fact that you and I rely on each other. We trust each other. We respect each other. When you have a problem, I listen. And you do the same for me. That is all I am speaking of. Is that not practical?" Sophie inquired.

"So let me give this a try," Sir Vival said. "When an employee successfully builds a relationship with a villager, if there is a problem, they work it out. They communicate, gather the facts and together find a solution. The conversation is always respectful. There is no blaming. There is an earnest desire to continue to do business together.

"When a good relationship exists, people feel welcomed to do business. They feel appreciated mostly because of the genuine way the employee interacts with them. And because you have built a relationship with the villager, she will give you a second chance. If someone else has the same goods for a cheaper price, she will still stick with you because you have invested in her."

"Remember, this is simple to understand, but not necessarily easy to do," explained Sophie.

"I hope our next meeting is soon," exclaimed Sir Vival. "You have helped Celelot survive in this competitive village environment."

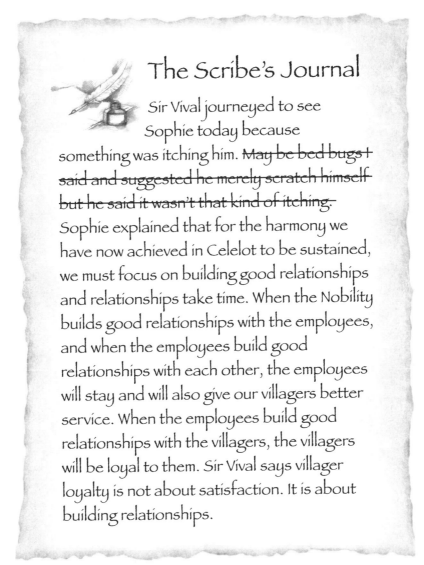

The Scribe's Journal

Sir Vival journeyed to see Sophie today because something was itching him. ~~May be bed bugs I said and suggested he merely scratch himself but he said it wasn't that kind of itching.~~ Sophie explained that for the harmony we have now achieved in Celelot to be sustained, we must focus on building good relationships and relationships take time. When the Nobility builds good relationships with the employees, and when the employees build good relationships with each other, the employees will stay and will also give our villagers better service. When the employees build good relationships with the villagers, the villagers will be loyal to them. Sir Vival says villager loyalty is not about satisfaction. It is about building relationships.

CHAPTER 15

FEELING SERVED

"Every Day is Villager Day in Celelot," Sir Vival read as he passed four posts on the way into the center of the town. He thought about the journey and how important Sophie's lessons were. He now knew that the most important element, the final piece needed for Celelot to survive and thrive consistently, was to focus on relationships.

Before going to the Castle, Sir Vival strolled through the town and thought about the subtle nature of what he needed to tell the King. The phrase, 'Build a relationship' sounded like some syrupy pudding—all sweetness, no nutrition.

Many times the most important lessons are lessons we resist, he thought. How could he get people to understand how important this lesson was? He thought about his own relationship with the King. The King had relied on him, trusted him, and confided in him. The King knew that Sir Vival had his and Celelot's best interest in mind. Sir Vival knew in his heart that if there was a foundational principle to villager loyalty, this was it. It was about relationships.

Sir Vival mounted his trusty steed and rode to the Castle. By now, all the guards and the servants knew him. He spoke to everyone as he made his way over the murky moat and through the Castle gate. He saw the King out in his garden and hurried over to him.

"My King, I wish to share with you the third and final step on our quest! The villagers will finally feel served."

"Go on," urged the King.

"When the villagers of Celelot feel that the employees have their best interest in mind, respectfully interact with them, are responsive to them, and seek to understand their needs, then the villagers will not leave.

"Being respectful, responsive and seeking to understand the needs of others builds good relationships. This is the last piece. Build good relationships with the villagers and it is likely that they will stay because they will *feel* served," said Sir Vival, pressing the palm of his hand over his heart for emphasis.

"In this town, typically there was much indifference toward the villagers. If a villager made a request, there was no certainty that the request would be granted with a willing heart. Kindness and empathy cannot be demanded. When a positive relationship exists, these things are automatic. A good relationship is the opposite of indifference.

"Our employees represent Celelot. They can choose to simply perform a transaction with the villager or choose to make the villager feel served by building a relationship. Therein is the difference between losing and winning, between surviving and dying. It makes the puzzle complete."

"Sir Vival, I hear you," replied the King. "My Queen and I have had offers to govern other kingdoms but we declined because we felt good here. We had developed relationships that we were unwilling to let go of easily. We must commit to doing the things we need to do to develop a relationship with our villagers, and to make sure our villagers feel served by us as we feel served by them."

"Listen and act on the feedback; begin inside out; build relationships—when we do these things our villagers will *feel* served," said Sir Vival. "This is the solution."

"Thank you once again, Sir Vival," said the King. "I am forever indebted to you."

And so it came to pass that in the Village of Celelot, King Stewart III and Queen Jennifer garnered a reputation for their welcoming ways. The town flourished as villagers from near and far chose to settle there. The village was noted for its extraordinary festivals, with elegant cuisine, fostered by the fine-tasting fruits and vegetables and the culinary artisans who prepared them. The King enthusiastically invited visitors to his village and ceremoniously slapped them on their backs. Most recovered and enjoyed their time in Celelot, although many avoided any additional contact with His Majesty.

Sophie remained in her own little world, as quiet and eccentric as she ever was. She became more respected as her input into the solution of the leaving villagers became known. Sophie started a little club that met by her big oak tree. She named it Green Space. Its members rallied for keeping armor and smelting waste out of the rivers and lakes of Celelot.

The King once more asked the Census Taker to perform his services to prove the town was growing again. This time, he went directly to Pearl who confirmed that fact. After his last loyal act, the Census Taker was rewarded by his King who held a banquet in his name. Many other villages tried ineffectively to recruit the Census Taker. One of them was the village located by a huge waterhouse, which offered him a good price for his services. But he stayed true to Celelot.

The Nobility planned daily strolls just to be with and speak to the villagers. But more importantly than chatting with them, they queried them about how happy they were. Upon hearing a troubling issue, they quickly acted upon what they learned.

The employees of Celelot, true to their role as ambassadors of their village, built relationships with their villagers and with each other. They knew they were an important key to keeping villagers in Celelot.

And Sir Vival went back to his garden, eager to put his hands into the rich soil of Celelot once more. The exquisite display of flowers adorning his property was said to be more the progeny of his creative mind than the result of his green thumb. He was forever finding new ways to make his plants bigger and better.

Sir Vival and Sophie kept in touch, engaging in the exchange of ideas that they loved so much. Together they created a vision, a vision of what Celelot could someday grow to be. Sir Vival did this because he was certain that one day he would again be called upon to be of service to his King. And he was determined to be ready.

The riddle solved in Celelot is a never-ending one. It is the battle of arrogance versus openness, the challenge of might versus right, the contest of indifference versus caring. It is the important quest for survival.

The Scribe's Journal

Sir Vival told me to end my
journal with a few important
things. He says that the villager is the only
one who matters and the only one who
has ever mattered in our village's success.
He also says that there are three steps to
make our villagers feel served. We need to
(1) systematically listen to our villagers and
act upon what we learn; (2) build an internal
environment of trust and respect with
employees (that's the inside out thing); and
(3) build relationships. When we do these
things, our villagers will feel served, and likely
remain loyal villagers.

The Scribe's Final, Final Entry

The process that worked:

√ Listened comprehensively to the villagers and acted upon what we learned

√ Listened comprehensively to the employees and acted upon what we learned because service begins inside out

√ Worked on building good relationships with villagers because where there is a relationship, the villager will give us a second chance

√ When we did these things, our villagers felt served. When this happened, our town prospered once again.

√ ~~Oops~~—forgot one thing. We took the census before and after so we knew if our solutions were working.

Your Faithful Scribe. ~~Duty done~~.

~ The End ~

The Scribe's Discussion Guide

I have been on a journey with Sir Vival to save the Village of Celelot and desire to engage you and your team in a thoughtful discussion about the matters in this manuscript. I have been a faithful scribe and recorded the events of note. The pieces in between however, are where some of the learning lies. Remember what Sophie said: "Wisdom cannot be received; it must be discovered."

Scribe's Discussion Guide

1. How does your organization currently demonstrate its commitment to service excellence? Be specific in terms of actions and behaviors.

_____

_____

_____

_____

_____

_____

2. How does your organization listen to its customers?

_____

_____

_____

_____

_____

_____

_____

3. How would you describe the differences between "getting served" and "feeling served?"

_____

_____

_____

_____

_____

_____

_____

4. Site an example of a time when one of your customers "felt served." What actions led to this? Site an example of when one of your customers "got served" but did not "feel served." What actions led to this?

_____

_____

_____

_____

_____

_____

_____

_____

5. On a scale of 1-5, how would you rate your internal customer service and **why?**

   5 Super

   4 Good

   3 Mediocre/Inconsistent

   2 Needs significant improvement

   1 Dreadful

   _____

   _____

   _____

   _____

   _____

   _____

6. Identify three specific ways to improve your internal customer service.

   _____

   _____

   _____

   _____

   _____

   _____

7. To build relationships with customers, an organization must be committed to a **consistent** level of excellent service. What are your roadblocks to a **consistently** high level of service?

8. Identify five specific things your company can implement, do more of, do less of or change, in order to build better relationships with your customers.

9. Great customer service is not an initiative; it is a commitment that is demonstrated. It can be consistently sustained, when it is a system. Please discuss your organization's commitment to the following critical components of excellent customer service.

   - Measuring Customer Service
   - Listening to the Customer
   - Customer Service Training
   - Rewarding Employees for Exceptional Service
   - Making Everyone Accountable for Customer Service

   _____

   _____

   _____

   _____

   _____

10. Now, specifically define three *personal* changes you will make to improve your internal and external service to customers.

Now, What Do You Do?

The goal of this book is to give you the tools to improve your customer service. Here is a strategy to make this goal a reality.

1) Gather a group of people together to read and discuss the ideas in this book.

> ➢ Your Department
> ➢ Your Management Team
> ➢ Your Internal Committee Members
> ➢ Your Roundtable

2) Work through the questions in the Scribe's Discussion Guide at the end of the book and document your ideas.

3) Prioritize action items based on impact on customer service— not ease of implementation.

4) Decide who leads what and over what period of time.

5) Rinse and repeat.

Remember to:
- Stay with it. Consistently press to the goal.
- Talk about it. What we talk about, we bring about.
- Monitor it. Measure your success in as many ways as you can think of.
- Enjoy it. After a period of consistent excellent service, your service reputation will improve.

Want More?

If you enjoyed the ideas in this book and would like Joan Fox to speak to your team, company or organization, email her at joan@joanfox.com or call 513-793-9582.

If you would like additional "Sir Vival" resources to make your customers "feel served" go to www.feelserved.com.

If you would like to give feedback to the author or share your success stories, email Joan at info@joanfox.com.

For a quantity book purchase discount schedule, visit www. feelserved.com.

Our Mailing Address is:

Eagle Inspiration Training & Development
PO Box 42754
Cincinnati, OH 45242

About the Author

Joan Fox is the founder of Eagle Inspiration Training & Development, Inc., a company whose mission is to increase the capacity of organizations to 'compete and win with service.' She is nationally recognized as a Customer Service Expert, partnering with clients who are serious about upgrading their customer service. Joan is a popular speaker and a sought-after consultant.

www.joanfox.com

www.feelserved.com